TURTLE RESCUE

TURTLE RESCUE

PAMELA HICKMAN

FIREFLY BOOKS

A Firefly Book

Published by Firefly Books Ltd. 2005

First printing

PUBLISHER CATALOGUING-IN-PUBLICATION DATA (U.S.)
(Library of Congress Standards)

Hickman, Pamela.
Turtle rescue : changing the future for endangered wildlife / Pamela Hickman. —1st ed.
[64] p. : col. photos. ; cm. (Firefly animal rescue)
Includes index.
Summary: Provides details and facts about turtles from around the world, their endangerment and extinction, and a range of conservation programs to save them. Includes profiles of individual conservationists and turtle species.
ISBN 1-55297-916-4
ISBN 1-55297-915-6 (pbk.)
1. Turtles —Juvenile literature. 2. Sea turtles—Juvenile literature. 3. Endangered species — Juvenile literature. I. Title. II. Series.
597.92 21 QL666.C5.H53 2004

LIBRARY AND ARCHIVES CANADA CATALOGUING IN PUBLICATION DATA
Hickman, Pamela
Turtle rescue : changing the future for endangered wildlife / Pamela Hickman.
Includes index.
ISBN 1-55297-916-4 (bound).—ISBN 1-55297-915-6 (pbk.)
1. Turtles—Juvenile literature. 2. Endangered species—Juvenile literature.
3. Wildlife conservation—Juvenile literature. I. Title.
QL666.C5H52 2004   j597.92   C2004-903043-4

Published in the United States by
Firefly Books (U.S.) Inc.
P.O. Box 1338, Ellicott Station
Buffalo, New York 14205

Published in Canada by
Firefly Books Ltd.
66 Leek Crescent
Richmond Hill, Ontario L4B 1H1

Design: Ingrid Paulson
Map: Roberta Cooke

The publisher gratefully acknowledges the financial support for our publishing program by the Canada Council for the Arts, the Ontario Arts Council and the Government of Canada through the Book Publishing Industry Development Program.

Printed in Singapore

TABLE OF CONTENTS

TALKING OF TURTLES

Imagine a creature that evolved 200 million years ago—before dinosaurs—and exists almost unchanged today.

The turtle has long been a part of creation stories, often representing the foundation of Earth. Native North Americans tell a story about a giant turtle floating in a primitive sea, with all the animals on its back. A Hindu tale describes the world as resting on the backs of four elephants that, in turn, stand on the shell of a turtle. For children today, the turtle stars in favorite stories ranging from *The Tortoise and the Hare* to the Franklin books.

Turtles carry the "slow and steady" label around with their shells, but a closer look reveals many surprises. There are about 270 turtle species in the world today. Large land turtles are commonly called tortoises, and the smaller freshwater species are referred to as terrapins. The sea turtle family includes the largest of them all, the leatherback. It has remained virtually the same for 20 million years, but is less than half the size of its ancient ancestor, the Archelon. A 70-million-year-old Archelon fossil found in 1996 measured 20 feet (6 m) wide at its front flippers.

Around the world, turtles are in decline. Parts of Southeast Asia have lost up to 80 percent of their freshwater turtles in the past 10 years, thanks to an unending demand for food and traditional Chinese medicine. Habitat destruction, pollution, fishing nets and the pet trade are also threats. Every species of sea turtle is endangered.

The good news is that governments, scientists, conservationists and turtle lovers have rallied together. They are committing their expertise, time and money to save the most endangered species, and to control the factors that threaten others around the world.

Turtles have been around a long time. They are survivors. Having lived through the mass extinctions that wiped out the dinosaurs, they are now facing their biggest threat yet—people.

Turtles are found across the globe, except in the Arctic and Antarctic. They live in fresh water, in oceans and on land—in surroundings ranging from tropical rain forests to deserts.

THE STORY SO FAR

For centuries, the turtle has been a source of food and medicine, as well as a popular pet. Not until the mid-20th century did people begin to notice a decline in many species. In the 1990s, concern turned to alarm as reports flooded in about the millions of turtles lost from China and Southeast Asia. Some formerly common species have disappeared. In recent years, people have set up captive breeding facilities and rescue centers. But there's still a lot to do, and time is running out for many turtles.

∧ Thousands of turtles are accidentally caught in shrimp nets and drown every year. Turtle exclusion devices can be attached to nets so trapped turtles are able to escape.

1959 The Caribbean Conservation Corporation is founded in Florida. It will become the world's longest-running sea turtle conservation society.

1975 The western swamp turtle is one of the first species added to the Convention on International Trade in Endangered Species (CITES). This makes it illegal to export the turtle from its native Australia without a permit.

1986 Conservationists establish Project Angonoka, a captive breeding facility for the plowshare tortoise in Madagascar.

1987 A western swamp turtle rescue operation begins in Australia, with a captive breeding program established at the Perth Zoo.

1989 China opens its borders to trade, leading to a huge increase in the transport of wildlife. By 2000, an estimated 12 million turtles are sold each year in China.

1995 Hong Kong's Kadoorie Farm and Botanic Garden is transformed into a center for conservation and education. It becomes the key to survival for thousands of turtles siezed from illegal traders.

1996 The plowshare tortoise is officially classified as endangered.

The Chinese three-striped box turtle is one of the most endangered and valuable species in southeast Asia. An unproven claim that traditional Chinese medicine made from the turtle can cure cancer has led poachers to hunt for the few that remain.

1999 For the first time, a leatherback at sea is fitted with a satellite tag, which provides valuable information on the species' movements.

2000 All of Vietnam's tortoises and freshwater turtles are declared threatened. The Chinese three-striped box turtle is classified as critically endangered.

2001 The Hong Kong government seizes an illegal shipment of 10,000 turtles headed for food markets in China, raising concern over the Asian turtle crisis. The following year, 26 more species are added to CITES.

2002 Scientists report that the Pacific population of leatherbacks is fewer than 5,000, a decline of 95 percent since 1980. They estimate that the global population of adult females has dropped from 115,000 in 1982 to fewer than 34,000.

2003 The U.S. sets new rules requiring "turtle excluder devices" on shrimp trawlers. It is predicted that the laws will save the lives of thousands of sea turtles each year.

2005 Baby olive ridley sea turtles hatched on a Malaysian beach for the first time since the early 1990s. It's believed the female laid eggs shortly after the 2004 tsunami, while the normally crowded beach was abandoned due to the disaster. Conservationists are campaigning to protect the beach area for future turtle nesting.

BUYING AND SHELLING

Since 1989, millions of freshwater turtles and tortoises have been shipped to China. There is a growing demand for their protein-rich meat and eggs in markets and restaurants: more than 10,000 tons (9 million kg) are eaten in China every year. And the animals' shells, bones and blood have been prized ingredients in traditional Chinese medicine for centuries. The critically endangered Chinese three-striped box turtles command up to $1,300 U.S. each, due to a recent (unfounded) report that they hold a cure for cancer.

Turtles are also popular pets. Asian species can easily be collected from market stalls and then sold as pets overseas. Suppliers pack the turtles so poorly that disease and dehydration kill the majority before they reach their destinations. The pet trades — both legal and illegal — are still very active. The rarer the species, the greater the demand and the higher the price.

Unfortunately, as Chinese turtle populations decline, the hunt has spread to the surrounding nations. Many people in these countries are poor, and the prospect of receiving hundreds of dollars for an illegal turtle is well worth the risk. Indeed, people in Vietnam claim they can trade a baby Chinese three-striped box turtle for a buffalo, while a rural villager in China can build a house with the money gained from an adult turtle.

Many freshwater species are now raised on farms, and in time these may become the main source of turtle meat, shell and bone in Asian markets. A steady supply of farmed turtles should keep costs stable, and hunters may be less likely to go after wild turtles when prices don't justify the effort. However, conservationists have learned that many markets claiming to sell farmed turtles actually get them from the wild.

∧ Millions of turtles are sold in Chinese markets for food and medicine.

< These green turtles are being farmed in the Cayman Islands to supply the huge demand for turtle meat around the world. Farming may help reduce the destruction of species in the wild.

TURTLE TERRITORY

Turtles can survive in only very specific areas. Each species has different needs—temperature, rainfall, food supply, predators and nesting places are all factors—and even slight changes in their habitats can wreak havoc. All of this means that turtle populations are usually tightly crowded, and spreading out to nearby areas is not always possible.

Turtles are predictable. When they find suitable habitat, they stay there. Even migratory species, such as sea turtles and some river turtles, follow regular routes and head to the same nesting beaches over and over again, which makes life easy for turtle hunters. When a population is discovered, hunters visit the area regularly until their traps come up empty. As one population is wiped out, hunters simply move on to another, and then another.

A turtle is an easy target.

Luckily, some turtles blend into their habitats. Their mottled green and brown shells make them hard to spot among the vegetation. But once seen, a turtle is an easy target. Even the slowest collector can catch a turtle on land, and the animals are easily netted in shallow water. Freshwater turtles—sometimes large groups of them—can often be found basking in the sun on rocks or logs in open, shallow water.

Many turtle hunters are amateurs, their traps simple. Some are box-like constructions of wire mesh and plastic chains. Others are holes dug into the ground and hidden with plants. Traps are visited every few days, turtles collected and bait replaced. Some hunters even leave their phone numbers, asking anyone who finds a trapped turtle to call and trade it for cash. Clearly, the risk of being caught isn't considered serious.

A group of red-eared turtles basks in the sun. Their tendency to group together in > open spaces and stay in the same space makes them easy to hunt or catch.

Cuc Phuong National Park is 136 square miles (350 km²) of rich tropical forest in Vietnam. It is also home to about 2,000 people, with another 50,000 in the surrounding buffer zone. It takes a lot of work to convince these people that harvesting trees, clearing land and hunting wildlife with no regard for conservation will lead to greater poverty down the road.

That's why the Cuc Phuong Conservation Project was set up in 1996. Its goal is to change people's attitudes toward the environment. Young people are often the most receptive, so Cuc Phuong's education program is working in more than 45 schools and 16 communities around the park. In addition, the park's 40,000 annual visitors receive on-the-spot education.

In 1998, Vietnam's first official turtle conservation project was born at Cuc Phuong, under the direction of American Douglas Hendrie. It began as a halfway house for turtles confiscated from illegal traders. The staff treats injuries and diseases and, when possible, the turtles are released into suitable habitat. So far, more than 400 turtles have been set free.

Inviting local people to bring in injured turtles and help care for captive ones encourages them to recognize the species at risk. It also builds support in the community for conservation. "The best way to ensure that turtles remain a part of Vietnam's heritage," says Hendrie, "is to protect the ones that still exist in their natural habitat."

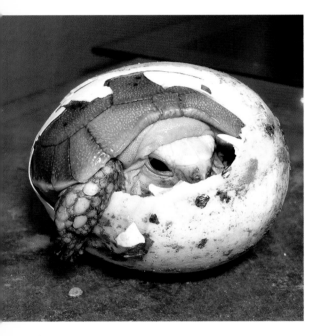

ʌ A baby turtle peeks out at the world for the first time. It is one of many that are hatched at the Turtle Conservation Centre in Cuc Phuong National Park, Vietnam.

Bui Dang Phong carries out field research on turtles at Cuc Phuong National Park using radio tracking.

Hendrie's program also encourages residents to report suspected illegal activities. This can be as simple as alerting authorities to someone seen with a sack of turtles. The project trains park staff, border patrols, police and others to stop illegal trade. After all, wildlife and customs officers must be able to tell one species from another. Proper handling of confiscated turtles also improves their survival rate.

You might not expect to see Vu Thi Quyen, one of Vietnam's top environmental crusaders, on a stage with the British Royal Family. But there she was in February 2001, accepting one of the world's premier conservation awards from The Princess Royal. Quyen has come a long way in a short time.

She studied at Hanoi National University in northern Vietnam. "Just before my graduation, my teacher introduced me to the Cuc Phuong Conservation Project. I applied and was accepted as the project's education assistant." Quyen quickly assumed more responsibilities, and today is considered a pioneer in conservation education, in not only Cuc Phuong but the entire country.

The key to her success has been putting responsibility in the hands of her staff, whom she encourages with rewards and a great sense of humor. "Because of her leadership," a colleague says, "the team has a professional pride and camaraderie that rival any I have seen anywhere."

Quyen feels that when local people are given an important role in conservation programs, they are motivated to make them a success. Because of this approach, authorities in her community are working to encourage better environmental practices, rather than simply trying to catch lawbreakers.

A turtle at Cuc Phuong Conservation Project. Our 40,000 visitors learn about turtle conservation at the project.

In 2001, Quyen founded Education for Nature–Vietnam (ENV), which sets up conservation programs in communities all over the country, and her methods have become a model for all of Southeast Asia. But time is running out. "Asia's turtle population is in trouble," she warns. "Loss of habitat and illegal trade have pushed many species to the edge of extinction."

Even people in the West can help protect Asian turtles, Quyen says. She asks that we don't buy turtles or products made from them, and that we spread the message to others. "Asian turtles urgently need help. It may be already too late for some."

BEACH BABIES

Like many people, diamondback terrapins prefer beachfront property. This species lives in the brackish (slightly salty) waters of the Atlantic and Gulf coasts of the United States, where freshwater rivers, creeks, marshes and bays meet the ocean.

All turtles lay their eggs on land. Each year during nesting season, female diamondbacks leave the water and climb onto beaches and sand dunes. Unlike birds, turtles do not defend or incubate their eggs—they simply lay them and leave them. However, in order to give their offspring the greatest chance for survival, females dig holes in loose sand, place the eggs deep inside and cover them carefully. The temperature inside determines the sex of the eggs: the warmer the nest, the more likely it is that the young will hatch as females.

∧ A sea turtle lays her eggs on a sandy tropical beach.

Like most turtles, diamondbacks return to the same nesting location year after year. Imagine their dismay when they find that sea walls, cottages, retirement homes and landscaped lots have replaced their sites. Do they give up? No way. These females, some of them 50 to 60 years old, head past the human obstacles as best they can and look for uncovered, loose soil above the high-water mark. Failing that, they dig in the loose edges of dirt roads and driveways. When a nest is far from the water, the babies must travel far to safety.

In the tropics, a female sea turtle must drag her weight—800 to 1,000 pounds (365 to 455 kg)—through the sand. It's not easy at the best of times, but when the beach is littered with broken fishing gear and other garbage, or piles of coconut husks and broken branches from storms, the turtle doesn't stand a chance. She may become exhausted trying to overcome the barriers. Then she'll either dig her nest too close to the sea—guaranteeing that the nest will be flooded—or give up and return to the water without nesting.

< Hatchlings are drawn to the ocean by its shine, but bright lights from buildings near the beach attract them away from the water. Stragglers may be eaten by predators or die from dehydration.

When you're an organization devoted to saving sea turtles, being around for almost 50 years means you're the most experienced conservationists on the beaches. But it also means that, despite decades of hard work, the turtles still need your protection.

∧ David Godfrey heads the world's longest operating turtle conservation group.

"The longevity of our programs is our greatest success, but also our greatest challenge," says David Godfrey, head of the Caribbean Conservation Corporation (CCC), which was founded in Florida way back in 1959. "Saving sea turtles and their habitat is a long-term venture. It's very hard to keep going, to keep raising the money. The work doesn't end."

Their hard work *is* paying off, though. CCC helped get sea turtles officially listed—and protected—as endangered species in the United States and internationally, and they're making sure countries such as Cuba, Cayman Islands and Japan do not resume the trade in hawksbills. They have eliminated turtle slaughterhouses in South America, and fought to protect breeding beaches for green turtles. In 2003, after years of lobbying, CCC and other environmental groups convinced the US to pass a law requiring shrimp trawlers to include larger holes in their nets, which will prevent thousands of unnecessary sea turtle deaths.

The group also wants to inform the public about the plight of turtles, so it has set up the Sea Turtle Migration-Tracking Education Program. People around the world can log on to the website and watch the migrations of individual leatherbacks, loggerheads and other sea turtles who have been fitted with satellite tags.

Hawksbill turtles are hunted for their beautiful shells.

The next 50 years for David Godfrey looks just as exhausting. "I'm optimistic because I can see that long-term conservation for sea turtles works. What's discouraging is there are still countries that want to reopen the turtle trade."

LIFE IN THE SLOW LANE

Sure, the tortoise in the fable outraced the hare, but there's no chance of the average turtle competing with a speeding car or SUV. Even its heavy shell can't protect it from an automobile.

So, why did the turtle cross the road? At nesting time, females are driven by instinct to climb out of the water and lay their eggs in the sand. When faced with condos and retaining walls, they keep going until they find a suitable site—often the soft shoulders of shore roads. In many regions, vehicles kill thousands of turtles each year.

Their lack of fear and slow—very slow—traveling speed make road-crossing success a long shot. The distances that some turtles must travel in order to nest—sometimes more than half a mile (1 km)—boggle the mind. Turtles are even victimized in protected areas like national parks: roads carved out of the wilderness for campers and hikers become attractive routes to female turtles on the move. Turtles that do survive their nesting trek are driven by instinct to return year after year, which increases their risk. And when the babies hatch, they too are faced with the immediate danger of dodging traffic in search of water.

Some turtles, it seems, have guardian angels. Volunteers in Cape Cod, Massachusetts, act as crossing guards for diamondbacks, marking their nesting sites for future observation and ensuring the females' safe return to the sea. In Nebraska's Valentine National Wildlife Refuge, the government put up a fence more than 5,000 feet (1.5 km) long near a breeding area of Blanding's turtles. The fence is designed to direct the animals under road culverts so they can safely get to the other side. All turtles should be so lucky.

This sign is a warning to motorists to be on the lookout for female sea turtles > that may wander across the road in search of a nest site.

Most people just drive by roadkill and pretend not to see it. Not Roger Wood. Every day, he collects and documents road-killed diamondback terrapins around the salt marshes of New Jersey.

Wood is a zoologist at Richard Stockton College, and founder of the Terrapin Conservation Project. In 1989, soon after learning about the large numbers of terrapins lost to traffic, he discovered that many of the dead females contained viable eggs. He and his volunteers removed some eggs, placed them in incubators at the college and waited 60 days until they hatched. The tiny hatchlings were released in nearby saltwater marshes—and quickly gobbled up by gulls.

He tried a new tack the following summer. The hatchlings were overwintered on a special diet and released the following spring, when they were bigger than a mouthful and less vulnerable. Each year since then, his team has raised and released 200 to 400 hatchlings.

∧ A rescued egg is about to release a new baby diamondback terrapin.

The project now works in cooperation with the Philadelphia Zoo and the Wetlands Institute of New Jersey. Staff and volunteers, including high-school and college students from all over the country, care for the zoo's share of hatchlings—about 100 each year. The diamondbacks are a major focus of the zoo's summer camp program. Over a three-week session, middle-school children help care for the hatchlings and record data on their growth. When the time comes to release the babies, everyone is emotional, kids and adults alike.

The larger the baby diamondback is when it is released into the wild, the better are its chances of survival.

Wood has also developed a turtle excluder device (TED) to be placed on crab traps. Diamondbacks are attracted to the bait in the underwater traps, which can catch and drown them. Each year, about 11,000 turtles die in these traps off New Jersey alone.

The TED reduces the size of the trap opening so large terrapins can't get in.

Since the Terrapin Conservation Project began, Wood has seen a growing commitment from families living along the shore to help protect nesting sites. "The public in southern New Jersey is now far more aware of terrapin conservation than it was back in the 1980s," says Wood. The highway department even puts up Terrapin Crossing signs every May, just before the nesting season begins.

That's a good sign for the future.

SCRAMBLED EGGS

Turtle eggs taste good. At least they do to the many predators that dine on them when opportunity knocks. Although female turtles do their best to hide their nests— and a good rain helps to wash away the scent—skunks, foxes, coyotes and raccoons can still sniff them out, dig them up and clean them out.

Sea turtles, which reproduce every two to three years, increase their chances of breeding successfully by nesting an average of six times in one season. The western swamp turtle isn't as prolific. It nests once a year, laying only three to five eggs at a time. Because the species' range is so limited and nest sites are fairly close together, red foxes, dogs and cats can easily wipe out a year's worth of eggs. Diamondback terrapins are facing similar problems as nesting sites diminish. "Instead of predators having to rummage over 50 miles of shoreline to find terrapin nests, it's like they're going to a delicatessen," says one conservationist. "Everything's right there in one place."

Natural predators are bad enough, but non-native species—those brought to an area by humans—can be a greater danger. For example, African bush pigs have been introduced into Madagascar, where they have no natural predators to control their population. They have a taste for plowshare tortoise eggs and hatchlings, and are a serious threat to the survival of the species. Even other turtles can become problems. When non-native pet turtles or "rescued" turtles are released into the wild by well-meaning but uninformed people, they may out-compete native species for food and shelter.

Even when eggs do hatch, gulls, shorebirds and crabs often pick off the tiny turtles as they make their way to water. Sharks and other large fish patrol nesting beaches, awaiting the hatchlings. With all these threats, the chances of a leatherback baby making it to maturity are just one in 1,000.

Adults are less vulnerable, but when western swamp turtles estivate—"hibernate" over the summer—they can be dug out and eaten by predators. Because it takes years for turtles to mature, the loss of an adult is even more devastating than the loss of a nest full of hatchlings.

< A baby turtle makes a light snack for a vulture on a nesting beach in Costa Rica. The large number of eggs laid by female sea turtles helps to compensate for the high rate of predation.

Conservation biologist Eric Alcorn can find a silver lining in research results others might consider a disaster. For several years, he's worked on the nest monitoring program for the Nova Scotia Blanding's Turtle Recovery Team. When the 2003 results came in from Kejimkujik National Park—one of only three small populations in all of eastern Canada—he learned that 23 of the 25 nests were destroyed by unusually high water levels. "But it's our highest number of confirmed nestings to date," he enthuses. This is good news, after all.

An average Blanding's turtle would just fit on this page. Its high-domed, dark brown or black shell is flecked with yellow, and its throat and chin are bright yellow. The Nova Scotia population is completely isolated from the main Blanding's range around the Great Lakes in Ontario and the U.S. Estimated at less than 500, the population is split between the national park, private and commercially owned land.

Losing eggs and hatchlings is not uncommon. Both are routinely threatened by raccoons, skunks, short-tailed shrews, ravens and ants. Part of the Turtle Recovery team's efforts include monitoring nesting females and placing wire cages over nest sites to prevent predators from digging up the eggs. Nest flooding, as seen in 2003, is an unpredictable problem, as is low temperatures. If the nest drops below 72°F (22°C), the eggs won't hatch.

∧ Eric Alcorn weighs, measures and scans a Blanding's female, takes a blood sample and then enters the data into the records. Each newly discovered Blanding's is processed and returned to its habitat within 24 hours.

These two turtle nests, laid the same day, had very different fates. The Blanding's nest on the left was protected with a wire cage by the recovery team. The snapping turtle's nest on the right was dug up by a raccoon and the eggs were eaten.

Biologist Tom Hermann, one of the leaders of the Blanding's turtle team, has been studying the Kejimkujik population since 1987. But even he admits that the species isn't an ideal research subject. "The turtles can live for more than 70 years and take 20 to 25 years to reach maturity," he explains. So the team's efforts to save the species will not be measurable for decades. "Our objectives require long-term commitment."

Kejimkujik park staff have been telling the Blanding's turtle story to their visitors since 1970. Through guided walks, posters and children's programs, thousands of people have learned to identify the turtle and understand the need to conserve it. The education program has even led to the discovery of two new populations outside the park.

Whether more will be discovered in the future is anyone's guess. In the meantime, the Blanding's turtle project is helping this isolated group to hang in there. "I'm optimistic that the population won't be lost," says one team member. "It's a good news story."

EASY PICKINGS

A thousand pounds (450 kg) of meat is hard to ignore when it's just lying there in front of you. Unfortunately for leatherbacks and other sea turtles, they aren't ignored enough. Their huge size makes them an easy and desirable target for hunters. Females are butchered while they lay prone on the beach, laying their eggs. Then the eggs are dug up and taken for food too.

Leatherbacks get their name from the leathery texture of their shell, which is much softer than that of most turtles. Beneath their rubbery skin is a two-inch (5-cm) layer of oily blubber that keeps them warm in cold waters. The oil, used in cosmetics, is as highly valued as their meat.

Many nesting beaches are in developing countries, where the people's survival often depends on wild-caught food. Locals can also sell turtle meat and oil at market. Conservation is a low priority when one's family needs to be fed.

∧ Sea turtles are often seen as a good source of food. Here a group of men grill freshly-caught turtle meat on the beach.

Other sea turtles are exploited in different ways. The hawksbill's beautiful shell is highly prized; shells are carved, painted, crafted into gifts and jewelry or sold whole. At customs, many prized souvenirs have been confiscated from unwary tourists because they came from an endangered sea turtle.

Many poorer nations—with the help of international conservation groups—have set aside protected areas for their threatened wildlife. Yet government officials do not always enforce laws against killing and trading turtles. Some have even been suspected of selling confiscated animals to dealers. Above all, local people need an alternative source of income and food for poaching to really stop.

< A mass nesting of sea turtles attracts a group of workers who are busy packing 80,000 turtle eggs into bags for sale. This large-scale exploitation can wipe out a whole nesting season and lead to population declines in the future.

December 11, 2001, is etched into the minds of the staff at Kadoorie Farm and Botanic Garden. That's the day when Hong Kong authorities brought in nearly 10,000 confiscated freshwater turtles. It took staff two days to unpack and assess them, and it was clear that they would be unable to house and care for them all. They quickly turned to other turtle sanctuaries around the world, and more than half of the surviving turtles were shipped to new homes. The rest found refuge at the farm's Wild Animal Rescue Centre.

∧ Volunteers carefully pack turtles for shipping overseas. The turtles are sent to partner conservation facilities that have space and resources for rehabilitation and captive breeding.

Kadoorie Farm was first set up to help hundreds of thousands of poor farmers in the 1950s. Over the years it replanted barren land into a lush tropical habitat, and in 1995 officially became a center for conservation and education. While mammals and birds as well as reptiles call it home, freshwater turtles are taking center stage.

The Wild Animal Rescue Centre includes a reptile sanctuary, outdoor turtle pens, an indoor hot room for turtles and a veterinary hospital. It rehabilitates and, when possible, re-releases native species such as the Vietnamese leaf turtle and Asian brown tortoise, as well as houses turtles siezed by authorities. The staff also assists in captive breeding programs, both on site and in cooperation with other centers around the world.

One of the thousands of turtles that were confiscated by Hong Kong authorities from illegal traders in 2001. Although many died of disease or dehydration, several thousand turtles were saved through the efforts of the Wild Animal Rescue Centre.

In addition to the Wild Animal Rescue Center, Kadoorie Farm set up an Ecological Advisory Program. Staff work together to provide information on issues that affect Hong Kong's environment. They see themselves as environmental watchdogs.

Since that December day in 2001, the Wild Animal Rescue Centre has been put to the test and succeeded beyond expectations. But as one of its conservation officers says, "Like all rescue centers, you just don't know what tomorrow will bring."

NIGHT CRAWLERS

At first it is just a dark shadow in the night, hovering in the gentle swells at the edge of the beach. It may even be a log carried inland by the ocean current. It's not until she actually beaches that you know you're looking at a female leatherback on a mission.

Slowly, with painstaking determination, she begins her climb up the sandy slope toward the high-water mark. It's dark. She can't really see where she's going, but instinct has led her back to this beach for over thirty years. Thousands of her eggs have been left here alone to survive as best they can. Only a few of her hatchlings are still alive.

Like all sea turtles, she has flippers for legs—perfect in water, but not very effective on land. She can't walk, so she "swims" slowly through the sand, leaving a track like a monster-truck tire's. Up to an hour later, she starts digging. Her back flippers excavate a deep, narrow chamber in the sand. They take turns dipping into the growing hole, scooping up sand and pushing it aside. Her deep, hot breaths smell of jellyfish. There are tears in her eyes, but not because she is crying. It's a biological function that helps remove sea salt from her body.

The leatherback keeps digging until the nest is deep enough to escape the notice of the hungry crabs, wild pigs and dogs that roam the beach at night. She can't do anything about the poachers. She drops white eggs the size of ping-pong balls—often two or three in quick succession—into the nest. Occasionally a small, infertile egg is mixed in with the good ones. She won't stop until she is close to a hundred eggs lighter.

Now the sand begins to fly as she fills in the nest and attempts to hide her tracks. She uses her heavy body and huge plastron—the underside of her shell—to pack the sand back into place. Then, carving a new track, the giant sea turtle heads back to the shining ocean.

< A thousand pound female leatherback moves down a beach after laying her eggs. Watching sea turtles nesting is turning into a big tourist draw on some tropical beaches.

To people on the Caribbean island of St. Lucia, Jim Sparks is known as Papa Turtle.

Animals have always been part of Sparks's life, but it wasn't until 1984 that he fell for the leatherback. "It was one of the most emotional experiences I have ever had," the veteran volunteer says. "To see an animal that has been around for 100 million years struggle up that beach to ensure that her species survived, and to know that man could drive her to extinction in a few short years, moved me more than you know."

∧ Volunteers monitor the number of eggs each female lays during nesting season.

The next year, Sparks began leading locals and tourists on Saturday-night turtle watches. Since then, he has continued to give up his weekends (and sleep) to help St. Lucians experience their wildlife and understand the need to conserve it. Turtle watches that began with five or six people have grown to include as many as 100.

In 2000, Jim launched a program, together with St. Lucia's fisheries department, near the biggest nesting beach of Grand Anse. Fourteen young people from the neighboring village now lead turtle-watch groups, at least four nights a week during nesting season. The community is more committed than ever to protecting leatherbacks, and participant fees bring much-needed money into the village. The turtles are safer, too, since the beaches are patrolled more often.

Although leatherback numbers in the Pacific Ocean have dropped drastically, Jim has seen them rise on St. Lucia's beaches. "They have increased from five per year in 1985 to as many as eight per night in 2002."

Jim's greatest reward has been teaching St. Lucian kids about respecting wildlife. "I have seen some of the children grow up to be teachers, or to work in forestry and fisheries. A few are also studying marine biology as a result of going on watches with me."

When people see a turtle in an unusual situation, they know whom to call. "One night a leatherback started laying near a local resort," Sparks remembers. "A young man stopped people from going near the turtle and called the police. They called me and I got there just after she had gone back in the water. The man had taken pictures of the turtle with his digital camera. When we asked him how he knew what to do, he said he had learned it from me on a turtle watch!"

∧ (top) Local Caribbean children learn about endangered leatherback turtles while on a turtle-watch outing. (bottom) A tag is attached to the turtle's front flipper so it can be identified if it is encountered again.

LONG LIVE THE TURTLE

The western swamp turtle and diamondback terrapin can live about 50 years, and the plowshare tortoise many more. Sea turtles have a life expectancy longer than people. Avoiding predators over such a long lifetime takes a combination of survival instincts and luck. Avoiding death by humans is becoming increasingly difficult.

In animals with long life spans, the juvenile stage tends to be long as well. The western swamp turtle doesn't reach breeding age for 10 to 15 years, and it's at least 20 years for a plowshare tortoise. So for every breeding turtle that is killed, it takes a decade or two for the population to recover.

For conservationists, a turtle's long life brings further challenges. The most common measure of a population's health is its nesting success. Scientists record the number of sea turtles nesting on any given beach, and of nests that hatch successfully, and compare these numbers from year to year.

But these results are only telling of mature females. There is no way of actually determining how healthy the juvenile females are, since they spend 10 to 20 years at sea before nesting. And males never return to land, so their population can only be estimated. If a juvenile population suffers a dramatic decline at sea, the alarm does not go off until many years later, when they begin to nest.

All of this leads to a long wait for recovery. "If we take an action today," says biologist Tom Hermann, "the result isn't felt for the next 50 or 100 years."

∧ Keeping eye on turtle nests is one way that researchers can reduce predation and poaching. Here, a game warden inspects a hawksbill nest in Borneo.

< The western swamp turtle is Australia's most critically endangered reptile.

The plowshare tortoise is one of the world's 10 most endangered reptiles. Named for the plow-shaped shell extension under the male's neck, the turtle has probably never been widespread, but is now restricted to just four small scrub forests. It lives on the northwest coast of Madagascar, in an area known as Baly Bay.

In 1986, conservationists set up a captive breeding center in what is now Ankarafantsika National Park. Seven plowshare tortoises—known locally as angonoka—were moved here from another location, and others confiscated from illegal traders were added to make up a breeding population. This was the beginning of Project Angonoka.

Captive breeding was considered the way to go. The declining tortoise population, estimated at between 100 and 400, is threatened by a variety of pressures in the wild. Until these problems can be sorted out, preserving the species in a protected setting makes sense.

The main threat to the tortoise is habitat destruction. When farmers burn undergrowth so they can graze their livestock on the shoots of new grasses, the habitat becomes unsuitable for angonoka. The tortoise is already confined to very small areas, and these further losses are pushing it toward extinction.

The angonoka is also threatened by wild pigs. These animals were introduced from Africa and have no natural predators on the island, so they are free to roam and multiply. (Malagasy, the native people of Madagascar, do not eat pigs.) They dig up turtle nests and eat the eggs as well as tiny hatchlings. Fencing off protected areas and caging nest sites seems to be the best defense.

< Plowshare tortoises are safe in the captive breeding center in Madagascar's Ankarafantsika National Park.

^ A tortoise breeding station at Project Angonoka.

Angonoka have been a part of Malagasy culture for centuries. Although the people follow a taboo against eating tortoises, they keep angonoka at home to protect their chickens and bring good luck. The tortoises are also highly prized in the pet trade, and poaching is another serious threat.

Since beginning its captive breeding program, Project Angonoka has set up a protected area at Baly Bay that supports about 1,000 tortoises. Researchers study the tortoise and the habitat, and the staff teaches people about the need for conservation.

The project also respects the needs of villagers. "It's not enough simply to declare an area off-limits to people, and police the boundaries," explains Lee Durrell of the Wildlife Trust. "Wildlife will still be hunted or traded by hungry people, or greedy people, or even just ignorant people. Working with the population to protect the species is more likely to be successful." Indeed, local people have taken on some of Project Angonoka's work, such as building firebreaks.

It hasn't all been good news for the center. Disaster struck in 1996, when thieves broke in and stole 73 juvenile and 2 adult female angonoka—the product of 10 years of hard work. It was a huge blow to the program, and worse, the crime went largely unpunished.

The successful captive breeding of angonoka is the key to saving the species from extinction. Babies like this one must survive for 20 years before they are ready to breed and contribute to a growing population.

Despite the setback, the first five captive-bred tortoises were released in 1998, and radio-tracking equipment has allowed scientists to monitor them in the new Baly Bay National Park. The future of the species depends on the continued success of the captive-bred population, and on the protection of reintroduction sites. The work will take decades. When it comes to helping a species that takes 20 years to reach breeding age, patience is a virtue.

TAKING THE BAIT

What looks like a jellyfish, floats like a jellyfish, and can kill a 1,000-pound (450-kg) turtle? A plastic grocery bag.

Leatherbacks are often tricked by floating plastic bags, mistaking them for food. Once they realize their error, they can't spit the bags out. That's because their mouths and throats are lined with backward-pointing spines designed to keep slippery jellyfish from escaping. (Adult leatherbacks can eat their own weight in jellyfish each day.) Even if a turtle doesn't choke, a bag can block its digestive tract and prevent it from feeding normally. One of the largest leatherbacks ever recorded was found dead on a beach with over 30 square feet (2.8 m²) of plastic in its gut.

Turtles also fall victim to fishing gear. In search of swordfish and tuna, longline fishers set as many as 10 billion hooks a year in the Pacific Ocean. A longline can run up to 60 miles (100 km) across the ocean's surface and dangle as many as 3,000 baited hooks at a variety of depths. About 40,000 sea turtles, attracted by the bait, die on these hooks each year.

During the winter of 1999–2000, about a hundred diamondback terrapins were found dead on the shores of Wellfleet Bay Sanctuary in Massachusetts. They showed no signs of trauma, injury or poisoning. It turned out that "ghost nets"—broken or discarded shellfishing drift nets—had been responsible. The turtles had been driven into pieces of underwater netting by tides, and were unable to escape.

Shrimp nets are one of the main causes of sea turtle deaths. When turtles get caught up in the vast nets—some big enough to hold a dozen jumbo jets—there's little hope of escape. A sea turtle has no reverse gear, so backing out of the net is not an option. There are escape hatches, but adult sea turtles are too big to fit through them. Leatherbacks can hold their breath for 15 minutes or so, but then drown. The U.S. shrimp industry accidentally kills about 2,300 leatherbacks each year.

< Turtles face many dangers at sea including broken and discarded nets from the fishing industry. Many turtles die after becoming tangled up in an underwater net since turtles can only hold their breath for a short time.

PLAYING TAG

Why is Canadian astronaut Bob Thirsk working with sea turtles? His project, Space for Species, tracks the migration routes of endangered animals from high above our planet. Researchers attach a tag—actually a mini computer—to a turtle's shell, so that the animal can be tracked all over the globe by satellite. One leatherback, tracked for 18 months, traveled from Trinidad to the North Atlantic, then down the west coast of Africa!

By combining this data with satellite images of turtle habitats, biologists hope to predict problems before they arise. The data also provides important information about turtles' home ranges, winter sites and routes followed. All of these details are vital to a species recovery plan.

There are more down-to-earth ways of keeping track of turtles. Tiny microchips can be injected into the shoulder muscle of a nesting turtle. Numbered metal or plastic clips can be attached to the edge of a sea turtle's flipper. The shells of smaller turtles are marked with a unique number and pattern of file notches.

During nesting season, volunteers recapture marked turtles, then measure, weigh, examine and photograph them. Some individual turtles can be followed for decades, giving researchers valuable information about a population's growth patterns and numbers.

∧ This space age turtle is helping scientists discover migration patterns and habitat use. The small pack on the turtle's back transmits signals to a satellite and allows the turtle to be tracked for many months.

Aman cruises down the highway in a roadster, a female at his side. But this female is a large diamondback terrapin, there is a box of hatchlings in the trunk and the man has just given high-school students a talk on turtle conservation.

His name is Don Lewis, and he's the mover and shaker behind the diamondback conservation work at Wellfleet Bay Sanctuary in Massachusetts.

Lewis, a former business executive, retired early and moved back to his roots on the shores of Cape Cod. His home is next door to the wildlife sanctuary, so he walked over one day to see if he could help. When offered a volunteer job working with terrapins, he answered, "Sure . . . er, what's a terrapin?" That was in 1999. Today, Don is the local expert, busy teaching students, homeowners and anyone else who will listen about the plight of this threatened species.

One of the terrapin's biggest problems is the blocking of its nesting beaches by sea walls, homes, landscaped lawns and other human-made structures. Lewis helps local residents understand that little things—like leaving driveways unpaved—can make a huge positive difference for the turtles. "Most people, given the opportunity, are more than willing to make the improvements," he says. In return, he makes sure that homeowners are present when terrapin eggs hatch on their property. And he puts a hatchling into the hand of each resident along the bay. After such a close-up meeting, people are usually hooked.

∧ Don Lewis is a full-time volunteer, dedicated to helping diamondback terrapins in any way he can.

When not down at the shore rescuing turtles, Don Lewis teaches terrapin research techniques to marine science students.

Lewis has teamed up with a teacher to launch a program called Turtles in the Classroom. At a recent lecture to over 400 students and parents, he reached into his bucket and pulled out an egg rescued from a maggot-infested nest. The egg had begun to crack. He instructed a student volunteer to hold the egg in her warm hands, and before he had finished his talk, a tiny new diamondback had hatched. Another turtle was added to the population—and several hundred terrapin enthusiasts were added to Don Lewis's growing following.

CAPTIVE BREEDING

David Galbraith, of Ontario, Canada's McMaster University, firmly supports captive breeding programs for threatened animals. But he's frustrated that they're needed at all. "They are clearly emergency responses, and they can only be temporary," he says. "Conservation should really happen in the wild. The fact that botanical gardens and zoos have become a last resort for critically endangered species is an indication of the failure of society."

Breeding endangered species of turtles in rescue centers, zoos and other facilities can make sense, particularly if their habitats are also threatened. Often, turtle programs are set up, in times of critical need, to house and treat confiscated turtles. Breeding and reintroduction schemes develop from there.

Even with good intentions, though, captive turtles are not always reintroduced wisely. Some small centers, lacking money, take short cuts. Turtles released without the proper health checks can introduce diseases into wild populations—with disastrous results.

Many zoos are now operating successful breeding programs, thanks to their expertise with captive animals and fundraising know-how. In addition, turtle experts around the world—breeders, veterinarians, scientists—have formed information- sharing networks. Together they breed thousands of threatened turtles, whose descendants may one day be introduced into the wild, when conditions are right. It's a little like storing your furniture until you have a place to live.

∧ Dean Burford weighs western swamp turtle eggs at the Perth Zoo in Australia. Without the zoo's captive breeding program, the turtle could now be extinct in the wild.

< At the Green Sea Turtle Egg incubation station in Borneo, green sea turtles are bred in captivity for human consumption. Captive breeding may save some species from extinction, but it may also encourage a continuing market for turtle products.

In the 1980s, when the world population of western swamp turtles was down to fewer than 50, things looked bleak. But scientists with the Perth Zoo weren't ready to say goodbye to Australia's most critically endangered reptile. They called on the zoo's Native Species Breeding Program for help.

The program breeds animals with the aim of releasing them into the wild. They also research how species reproduce, to help scientists with their recovery plans.

The zoo began a rescue operation for the western swamp turtle in 1987. In the first five years, its population grew from 17 turtles—including only three mature females—to 130. By 2000, over 300 western swamp turtles had been bred. It takes 10 to 15 years for a female to reach breeding age, so as more captive females mature, the offspring rate will increase. Between March and September of 2003 alone, 37 hatchlings were born.

The biggest obstacle for scientists now is in finding enough suitable habitat for the turtles. Western swamp turtles are presently confined to two very small swamps, which are officially protected as nature reserves.

Gerald Kuchling, of the University of Western Australia, has led an intensive western swamp turtle recovery program at the zoo since 1991. To make the most of its breeding and reintroduction efforts, the program monitors the species in the wild, and works to improve habitat and control predators. In its 2001–2002 season, 42 turtles were released into the wild.

∧ Dr. Gerald Kuchling is credited with saving the western swamp turtle.

The Perth Zoo successfully breeds western swamp turtles. The challenge is to find enough suitable habitat where they can be safely released into the wild.

In addition to its behind-the-scenes rescue efforts, the Perth Zoo, like many zoos around the world, educates thousands of visitors each year. Children and adults can observe the western swamp turtles on display, learn about their plight and discover how they can help the species on its road to recovery.

WHAT IS THE TURTLE'S FUTURE?

Fossils reveal that turtles have been around for millions of years. But it's new data—showing a dramatic decline in numbers, particularly in Southeast Asia—that has conservationists alarmed. Turtles are facing the greatest challenge of their evolutionary history. But there are many people who are fighting hard to save them.

Like Gerald Kuchling, who is spearheading the recovery of the western swamp turtle in Australia. And Don Lewis, who wades into frigid water to rescue cold-stunned diamondback terrapins. And Roger Wood, who picks up road-killed turtles to save their eggs. These are just some of the extraordinary individuals who are making a difference. There are many others fighting on behalf of the world's turtles. But will it be enough?

Time alone will tell. Conservation programs may not see real results for half a century or more. What we do know is that we must stop illegal trade and poaching, and we must protect and restore turtle habitat. We need new laws that will reduce ocean pollution and stop accidental trapping and hooking by fishing boats.

Critically endangered species can be sustained by rescue centers, zoos and private breeders until it is safe for them to go back to the wild. How long that will take is up to governments, conservation groups and individuals.

Bringing a species back from the edge of extinction takes time. It is up to all of us to ensure that slow and steady wins the race.

FAST FACTS

Scientific names
- approximately 270 species, making up 12 families in the reptilian order Testudines

Size
- species range from the mud turtle, at about 3 inches (7.6 cm) long, to the 7-foot (2-m) leatherback, weighing over 1,000 pounds (450 kg)

Life span
- small turtles may live for up to 50 years; large sea turtles and tortoises likely live 100 years or more

Shell
- textures range from the hard carapace (upper shell) of tortoises and typical freshwater turtles, to the soft leathery covering of leatherbacks, to soft-shelled, pancake-like turtles
- plastron (underside of shell) may be hinged, allowing the turtle to pull in its neck, head and legs for protection

Locomotion
- terrestrial turtles, like tortoises, have thick, stump-like legs for walking; front legs may be flattened for digging
- freshwater turtles are expert swimmers with webbed feet, but can also walk on land when necessary
- sea turtles' legs are modified into flippers for swimming

Reproduction	• all turtles lay shelled eggs on land; eggs are buried and left alone
	• small turtles mature in five to 10 years; sea turtles as many as 30
	• eggs number from two or three per year for some species, to 600 or more every two to three years for a leatherback
Diet	• no teeth; sharp beaks are used to bite off plants or crush insects, fish, small birds, amphibians and small mammals
	• most sea turtles feed on plants and invertebrates such as sponges; leatherbacks prefer jellyfish
Seasonal activity	• sea turtles and some river turtles migrate between feeding grounds and nesting beaches; longest recorded trip by a leatherback over 3,600 miles (5,800 km)
	• in cold climates, turtles burrow into muddy pond bottoms or leaf litter and hibernate
	• in hot, dry climates, turtles burrow underground or into leaf litter and estivate

HOW YOU CAN HELP

If you would like to learn more about turtles and the projects designed to protect them, contact one of the following organizations or visit their websites.

Canadian Amphibian and Reptile Conservation Network
www.carcnet.ca

Provides general information on turtles and conservation, including specific Canadian species such as Blanding's turtle.

Caribbean Conservation Corporation
www.cccturtle.org

4424 NW 13th Street, Suite A1, Gainesville, FL, U.S.A. 32609
Phone (800) 678-7853 or (352) 373-6641
Runs a sea turtle migration-tracking education program on the Web. Also offers the opportunity to adopt a turtle.

New York Turtle and Tortoise Society
www.nytts.org

P.O. Box 878, Orange, NJ, U.S.A. 07051-0878
Presents information on the Asian turtle crisis and the diamondback terrapin recovery project.

Space for Species
www.spaceforspecies.ca

Aimed at teachers and students in grades six to nine. Monitors migratory species and their habitats from space.

Traffic Indochina
www.trafficindo.org

c/o WWF Indochina Programme Officer, 53 Tran Phu Street, Hanoi, Vietnam
Discusses trade in endangered species, including turtles, especially
in Vietnam.

World Wildlife Fund Canada
www.wwf.ca

245 Eglinton Avenue East, Suite 410, Toronto, ON, Canada M4P 3J1
Phone (888) 26-PANDA or (416) 489-8800
Includes information prepared especially for kids and teachers.

World Wildlife Fund US
www.worldwildlife.org

1250 Twenty-Fourth Street NW, P.O. Box 97180,
Washington, DC, U.S.A. 20090-7180
Phone (800) CALL-WWF
Presents the WWF's work in preserving wild places, saving endangered
species and addressing global threats.

INDEX

PHOTO CREDITS

AUTHOR'S NOTE

I would like to dedicate this book to my family.

I have discovered a world of extraordinary turtle conservationists while researching this book. I wish to thank them for sharing their knowledge and time, and for working so hard on behalf of the world's declining turtle populations. Special thanks go to Jim Sparks, Don Lewis, Roger Wood, Vu Thi Quyen, Douglas Hendrie, Thomas Hermann and Eric Alcorn. I would also like to express my appreciation for my editor, Dan Bortolotti, for his help and expertise.

Thanks also to Cliff Drysdale, Ron Fricke and David Godfrey.